OTHER BOOKS BY SERPENT CLUB PRESS:

Autumn, Again; Spring, Anew
Michael Skelton & Stephen Morel

A Quarter Century
Eda Gasda

Circumambulate
Daniel Bossert

Moon on Water
Matthew Gasda

New Writing: Volume I

New Writing: Volume II

On Bicycling: An Introduction
Samuel Atticus Steffen

Sonata for Piano and Violin
Matthew Gasda

The Substitute
Michael Skelton

ARDOR

A play by Matthew Gasda

SERPENT CLUB PRESS

ARDOR

Copyright © Serpent Club Press, 2016

All rights reserved

Serpent Club Press books may be purchased for educational, business, or sales
promotional use. For more information please contact Serpent Club Press at
theserpentclub@gmail.com

First Edition

Printed in the United States of America
Set in Williams Caslon   *
Designed by Emily Gasda

ISBN
9780997613421

ARDOR

An original drama
by Matthew Gasda

ARDOR had its world premiere at Saint Mary Magdalen Orthodox Church in New York City. Opening night was on November 4th, 2016 (Di Di Chan, Bronwyn Kelly, Matthew Gasda, Producers). The production was directed by Matthew Gasda; the set design was by Jacqueline Brockel; the costume design was by Ashley Owen; lighting design was by Joseph Magnus; the stage manager was Allison Boenig. The cast was as follows:

Alana ....Anamari Mesa
Andre ....Greg Petroff
Arthur ....Xavier Burak
Charlie ....Vincent Santvoord
Chloe ....Melissa Nelson
Fred ....Ladi Akinwande
Leo ....Tad D'Agostino
Sophia ....Makaela Shealy
Victoria ....Kim Sweet

Characters:

[Ages at the beginning the play]

Alana, *a dancer, 24*
Andre, *a painter, Chloe's Uncle, 55*
Arthur, *a mystery, 22*
Charlie, *a playwright, 24*
Chloe, *a musician, 24*
Fred, *a writer, 24*
Leo, *an actor, Chloe's younger brother, 19*
Sophia, *Andre's art model, 19*
Victoria, *a theater director, 24*

Setting:

A large room in Andre's farmhouse with a large, round table, a feinting couch, a larger sofa, an antique rocker, oversized black chair a coffee table, an easel, and a bookshelf. There is also an old upright piano and a guitar propped against the piano. There are several exotic rugs. The wings of the stage represent doors and hallways leading to other parts of the house: kitchen to the left, bedrooms to the right. A door at the back center of the stage represents the door leading to the outside.

ACT I

The stage is dark.

The stage brightens, signifying daytime.

Enter Andre and Sophia.

Andre goes to the easel and begins to prepare paints for his canvas. Sophia assumes a pose on the fainting couch.

The light begins to dim to mark the waning of the day.

Andre switches on artificial light, to mark the beginning of night.

Enter Leo, Fred, Victoria, Chloe, Alana, who arrange themselves in the common room of a spacious, bohemian farm-house.

They open wine bottles and begin to pour.

CHLOE
In some ways, I only hear words once they break me.

FRED
You're misconstruing what I said—

VICTORIA
No she's not.

CHLOE
I weigh my thoughts until they're tied around my wrists.

VICTORIA
There's an urgency to getting older that's uncomfortable. Suddenly every decision is attached to a consequence.

ALANA
I like it.

CHLOE
I don't. My bladder hurts.

LEO
Mom called today.

CHLOE
Why?

LEO
She wanted to talk.

CHLOE
About what?

LEO
She scheduled dental appointments for us, because she knew we wouldn't do it for ourselves.

CHLOE
Fuck that.

VICTORIA
Fred, I heard you've started writing letters to everyone...except for me.

CHLOE
Mom annoys the shit out of me.

FRED
I'll write to you, if you write back.

VICTORIA
I'd really like that.

LEO
She's losing sleep over our teeth—

CHLOE
She's pyscho.

FRED
My mom's the same way.

VICTORIA
So's mine.

ALANA
My parents are hippies.

CHLOE
I love your parents so much.

ALANA
They're more fun for other people.

CHLOE
Uncle Andre, can we all never go back to New York and stay here forever?

ANDRE
No sorry.

ALANA
Charlie sent me his new play—did anyone else read it?

VICTORIA
Can we not talk about him, please?

FRED
I read it.

ALANA
What do you think?

LEO
Based on the pained look on Fred's face...

ALANA
Yeah, it wasn't...great.

VICTORIA
Please guys. It's making me uncomfortable.

FRED
He's on his way up here by the way—

VICTORIA
Wait what?

CHLOE
We didn't want to tell you, or else you wouldn't have come.

VICTORIA
Fuck you all. Seriously. That's so screwed up.

FRED
It excites you.

VICTORIA
Of course it does.

FRED

So why are you pretending that you're angry?

VICTORIA

You took away my agency—

FRED

Agency's boring.

VICTORIA

Not to me.

LEO

I ran into Charlie a few weeks ago, he seemed kinda depressed.

VICTORIA

Someone probably, finally told him that he's got a small cock and the shock was too great—

CHLOE

Does he really?

VICTORIA

No, but compared to his ego, it's microscopic.

CHLOE

Leo, are you gonna go home at all this summer?

LEO

No.

CHLOE

I think I might. I miss cuddling with the dog. Aw.

LEO

You're ridiculous.

CHLOE

Don't you just want to hug him though? Aw. That little bunghole.

VICTORIA

Bunghole?

CHLOE

That's what I call the dog.

VICTORIA

Is that his name?

CHLOE
No, his real name is Calvin, but I think he's such a bunghole, so I call him Bunghole.

VICTORIA
Are you working on anything new?

ALANA
I'm rehearsing a new piece. We'll see.

LEO
Your last show was amazing.

ALANA
It was ok.

LEO
No dude: it was incredible.

ALANA
Thanks.

CHLOE
I'm sorry I missed it.

ALANA
It's ok.

CHLOE
I still feel guilty about it.

LEO
She got too high and paranoid to leave her apartment—

CHLOE
Leo, I tell you these things in confidence—

ALANA
It's no big deal—

CHLOE
It's embarrassing.

ALANA
Chloe, no one's judging you—

CHLOE

I want to write songs. I want to make films. I want to learn languages. Because I always end up farting around my apartment instead. Soul after soul after soul passes through my body, and none of them ever stick; so I can't ever figure out who I am...

ALANA

I love watching dust float in the lamp-light...

CHLOE

It's like, I always end up sending long text-messages to people trying to explain, and re-explain, and re-re-explain, what I tried to say in person—

ALANA

I have such good memories of the first trip we took up here, after freshman year—

VICTORIA

I think that was the summer I was bulimic...

CHLOE

Or the summer I was anorexic—

ALANA

I was just grateful to have cool people to hang out with.

VICTORIA

We were cool people?

ALANA

To me you were.

CHLOE

Do you know those Japanese paper flowers which recover their magical shapes once they've been dipped in water?—I feel like one of those flowers, in search of a pool of water to recover myself in.

ALANA

I read recently that flowers evolved color in order to attract insects to pollinate them. Which means that, if you think about it, nature needs beauty to survive.

CHLOE

I'm so jealous of this gift you have for articulating shit.

ALANA

I don't think it's a gift—

CHLOE

Then what is it?

ALANA

An accident.

VICTORIA

Chloe, you do realize that you're also uncommonly articulate—

CHLOE

On the subway every night, feeling half-empty. Buried in my phone as if it mattered. I feel like a dying spark.

VICTORIA

You see what I mean, right? Like, you hear yourself—

CHLOE

Personally, I've never been afraid of a low-key black-out while drinking—

ALANA

Why are we so ashamed of our emotions?

FRED

Because shame is a method of control.

ALANA

It's true...

LEO

But what if shame is the emotion and not the thing controlling the emotion? How do you know shame isn't all there is?

FRED

You don't.

ALANA

What are you ashamed of Leo?

LEO

At school I go to parties, get really wasted, and act like an asshole. It's my routine. It doesn't make me happy. And I have no idea why it happens. I don't know the person who's living my life for me—

CHLOE
Which means he fucks a lot of girls he doesn't care about—

ALANA
I thought you had a girlfriend?

LEO
We broke up.

VICTORIA
I'm gonna make some coffee, does anyone want some?

LEO
I do.

VICTORIA
Anybody else?

FRED
I'll have some.

CHLOE
Me too.

VICTORIA
Ok.

Exit Victoria.

ALANA
It's crazy that you're the age we were Leo, when we first started coming up here; I remember you being this super-annoying little middle-school kid who still thought the word 'poop' was funny—and now you're like this full-blown American adult male—

LEO
It's weird, right?

ALANA
We were all so passionate and self-absorbed and out of control at 19—and now 6 years later I realize that that kind of narcissism was the result of having failed to create a secure self-identity—but I wonder if it still is, I mean; a failure...

CHLOE

I think I'm gonna quit my job. It's at a restaurant. It's horrible. And I'm sleeping with my boss: a human I do not care for, but nonetheless am offering my youth and beauty to.

LEO

That sounds like such a bad idea Clo...

CHLOE

Sometimes I get drunk by myself and fall asleep in the bathtub, wake up, and go to work the next day still drunk.

FRED

Charlie's running late, he texted me.

Victoria returns.

VICTORIA

He's always running late.

FRED

He said traffic was bad getting out of the city.

CHLOE

You're freaking out—

VICTORIA

I'm not freaking out...it's just...he meant a lot to me. Shit, the coffee—

Exit Victoria.

CHLOE

Lately, I've been taking a lot of therapeutic salt baths lately, it's really good for my bladder. No one finds this interesting, do they? Being in your twenties sucks. Being broke, single, disrespected on a daily basis. Honestly. I smoke extra cigarettes just to look older.

Victoria returns, with coffee.

ALANA

You have such lovely skin though Chloe, it's a shame—

VICTORIA

I think I had a mini-panic-attack while I was waiting for the coffee to percolate...

FRED

I told you, I can ask him to—

VICTORIA

No, my pride forbids it.

FRED

Whatever you say.

VICTORIA

You think I'm being stubborn—

FRED

Well if you're going to get this upset about it—

VICTORIA

I'm not upset. I just haven't properly mourned him. So this what needs to happen actually. I need to talk to him.

FRED

In all seriousness though, are you sure you're ready to do that?

VICTORIA

Yes. Absolutely. Why?

FRED

Because when silence breaks into speech, it usually doesn't stop for a long time. Why do you think Shakespeare's characters are always, endlessly, talking? Because if they stop, then they have to face the fact that they're nothing but words on a page.

CHLOE

Such a writer thing to say.

FRED

But I can't write anything...

CHLOE

But you're such a writer anyway—

LEO

Does anyone want to go fishing tomorrow?

CHLOE

No.

CHLOE
I'm gonna go have a cigarette, does anyone want to join me?

VICTORIA
I'll go.

Exit Chloe and Victoria.

LEO
I actually went to see the first play Victoria and Charlie did together when you guys were undergraduates. It made a huge impression on me. I gave up a baseball scholarship to go to a conservatory and I'm like, pretty sure it was because I was in the audience that day. That play was sick: it ripped things open for me. My dad was so pissed at me, too—and he's still not over it, honestly. I committed a mortal sin in his eyes....By the way—my sister is a mess—

ALANA
Something's going on with her for sure.

LEO
She drinks, looks at the internet, drinks, goes to parties, takes long baths. That's every day for her, in some order. And she doesn't write songs anymore—

FRED
Kill everything to kill the silence—

ALANA
Is acting emotional for you Leo?

LEO
Sometimes.

ALANA
What about the times it's not?

LEO
What's your point?

ALANA
I dunno.

LEO

I went swimming this afternoon down at the creek, which is maybe like, a half-mile away. It brought back a lot of memories. Andre used to take Chloe and I there when we were little kids. We'd wear water wings and splash around all day. It was great. I'd float through pools of shadow and sunlight; watch the monarchs feed from the milkweed tufts…bees pollinate the wild echinacea growing along the creek-banks. I'd absolutely love to go back and live those days again. Man.

FRED

No you wouldn't: no one would relive childhood if they really thought about it.

ALANA

Leo, are you gonna tell us what happened with your girlfriend? You looked so happy in your pictures together…

LEO

Aw, I wish I hadn't said anything.

ALANA

Why?

LEO

Because I have literally zero desire to talk about it.

ALANA

What happened?

LEO

You heard what I just said right?

ALANA

Yeah, but I don't believe you.

LEO

No, but like, you should.

ALANA

Why?

LEO

Why?—because it's super private.

ALANA
Don't keep secrets.

LEO
It's so awkward.

ALANA
Who cares?

LEO
We broke up…because…no, never mind, I can't tell you.

ALANA
Leo—

LEO
I can't say it in front of my uncle.

ANDRE
I don't care.

LEO
Yeah but I do.

ALANA
Oh come on—

LEO
She said she wanted to try anal…and I said no, I didn't want to—stop laughing—and she got really offended and weird about it, and then I got weird about it and then—Andre stop laughing—it lead to this long conversation about intimacy in which we discovered that we didn't actually have any intimacy…at which point, she broke up with me.

FRED
Why didn't you want to try anal?

ALANA
Yeah, Leo, why?

LEO
It's dirty.

FRED
It's not dirty.

ALANA
Wait Fred: you've tried—

FRED
Sure.

ALANA
Wait really?

FRED
Yeah.

ALANA
I'd have never have guessed.

FRED
Why?

VICTORIA
You're too poetic.

FRED
Exactly.

ALANA
Was that a joke?

FRED
Yeah.

LEO
Alana have you done it?

ALANA
Me?

FRED
You've definitely done it—

ALANA
You guys watch too much porn; even I did, it's not like what you think.

FRED
I don't watch porn.

LEO
Yes you do—

16

FRED
  Nope.

LEO
  How?

FRED
  I just don't.

LEO
  But you've seen it right?

FRED
  Once or twice, a long time ago.

LEO
  Damn.

  Enter Victoria and Chloe.

VICTORIA
  What's so funny?

FRED
  Inside joke.

CHLOE
  What inside joke?

FRED
  We'd tell you but it's an…inside joke.

CHLOE
  Oh, I want to know!

LEO
  ANYWAY—

CHLOE
  Pleaaasssse.

LEO
  ANYWAY—

VICTORIA
  It's a beautiful night, by the way. You guys should go out on the porch.

FRED

I'm gonna go for a walk later.

CHLOE

Such a writer thing to say!

VICTORIA

You're obsessed with Fred tonight...

CHLOE

Fred's adorable—

VICTORIA

Fred I feel like I have no idea what's going on with your life...

FRED

I'm moving back in with my Mom.

CHLOE

Really?

FRED

Yeah.

CHLOE

Why?

FRED

Because I have no money and no job.

ALANA

I can't imagine you not living in the city.

FRED

I'm tired of it, honestly.

LEO

I feel like you're gonna write the next great American novel.

FRED

I'm not going to write anything. I'm just going to go home and stare out the window for the next ten or twenty years.

VICTORIA

What did you major in again? Creative writing?

FRED

Philosophy.

CHLOE

Ew. Why?

FRED

Because I think about my emotions at the same time that I feel them.

VICTORIA

That makes me uncomfortable.

FRED

It can't make you as uncomfortable as it makes me.

ALANA

I'm out here and my eyes are open and my consciousness is open and my heart is open and I'm listening, hoping—but I look at you, and there's something so closed.

FRED

When I was little, maybe four or five years old, a part of me used to think that I was waiting for permission from someone to die; I wasn't sure why exactly—it just seemed better to be dead; like in the same way that it's better to have an umbrella when it's raining than not to have one. I didn't even realize that it was unusual until I was older. But wanting to die makes other people uncomfortable, so I stopped. No one noticed, nothing changed on the outside. It was an external thing, a little click, like a machine changing gears.

CHLOE

You're gonna fill the whole room up with your gloominess.

FRED

Sorry.

CHLOE

I feel stressed out all of a sudden.

FRED

That's because you've been internalizing what everyone around you is feeling.

CHLOE

I wish you were capable of displaying your emotions in a way that was recognizable to other people Fred: that would be awesome.

LEO

I feel like it's time for everyone to smoke a joint—

VICTORIA

I don't think we're really in the mood.

LEO

Whatever, I'm gonna go smoke by myself then and fall asleep.
Goodnight everyone.

ensemble

Goodnight/gnight/gnight Leo.

Exit Leo.

CHLOE

Fred, let's go for a walk. I feel like we should talk.

FRED

Yeah, ok.

Exit Fred and Chloe.

ALANA

They're so into each other, they just don't realize it.

VICTORIA

Alana: how are you? I feel like we haven't talked since the funeral.

ALANA

Yeah, because I haven't been talking to anyone.

VICTORIA

Are you ok?

ALANA

I'm fine. It's the utter absurdity of moving on that gets me...

VICTORIA

I find it helps to lock the door, and talk to myself out loud until I
get upset and start crying, and then keep talking and crying...I'm
often surprised by what I say—

ALANA

That's not really my style.

VICTORIA

No problem.

ALANA

Don't judge me.

VICTORIA

I'm not judging you.

ALANA

Grief's like menstrual blood: clotted, burdensome--not lovely, not fresh.

VICTORIA

I'm sorry.

ALANA

It makes me so angry. I just want to be allowed to be angry.

VICTORIA

You're allowed—

ALANA

The innocent things in us are pulled out like teeth—aren't they?

VICTORIA

I'm starting this MFA in the fall and I don't really know why. I'm a good director, maybe even more than that…but I know that I've developed the awful habit of working for the sake of other people's praise—meaning that getting an MFA is probably the worst possible idea…

ALANA

You're overthinking it.

VICTORIA

You seem to be able to leave everything behind and let things be, but I can't: I drag my every-day-self into the rehearsal room, which means it's exhausting.

ALANA

I let things be because I have no choice. I can't dance heavy. I can only dance light.

VICTORIA

But there are these moments in the theater, in directing, where human nature begins to feel like water…I mean, I guess— sometimes the uncharted territory the heart ends up discovering is itself….I just don't like the way people are cut off from themselves; fast asleep. It gives me purpose to say: I can change that; I can wake people up. But like, on the other hand, I might one of the asleep people myself. Like, there's a part of me that's completely automated. My life is my own, I can leave my apartment in the middle of the night and walk around singing if I wanted to. But I never do. I mean, I never break routine.

ALANA

No one does—

VICTORIA

And I'm emotionally fixated on this person who doesn't care about me at all. Who's not in my life, at all.

ALANA

He's probably gotten fat and boring.

VICTORIA

I always told myself that I would never direct one of those plays where women just talk about men the whole time. So it's really devastating to hear myself and realize that I am one of those women….I think I need to go to bed.

ALANA

Ok. Goodnight.

VICTORIA

Goodnight Alana. I'm glad we got to talk.

Exit Victoria.

ANDRE

Something's in the air tonight.

ALANA

A collective quarter-life crisis.

ANDRE

Chloe told me about your girlfriend by the way. I'm sorry—

ALANA

It's ok.

ANDRE

Is it?

ALANA

It's just something to say. It's obviously not ok, or ever gonna be ok.

ANDRE

Do you talk about it with anyone?

ALANA

No.

ANDRE

A therapist or anything?

ALANA

No, no—I tried; but—it wasn't helping.

ANDRE

Why?

ALANA

Why? Because I just sat there silently while the shrink racked up billing hours.

ANDRE

So what are you doing to deal with that feeling?

ALANA

What feeling?

ANDRE

Overwhelming grief.

ALANA

I'm mostly numb. Numb to that fact that Catherine isn't coming back. But that just makes me aware of how numb everybody else is.

ANDRE

Death is a process that's happening all the time. When someone dies we become more aware of it, but it's always operating on one level or another—

ALANA

Is that why you paint?

ANDRE

I paint because this world is miserable and idiotic and mostly evil, and art is one of the few things that can't be reduced to all that bullshit—

ALANA

What do you do when people don't understand you?

ANDRE

No one understands anyone, we can only approximate understanding—

ALANA

Ok but when the approximation's really really off—

ANDRE

I never give a shit about what other people think, about anything.

ALANA

Sounds nice.

ANDRE

It is. But that's not my point.

ALANA

What's your point?

ANDRE

That the grief will eat you alive unless you do something about it.

ALANA

I'm just confused.

ANDRE

No you're not confused, you're lucid and that's why you feel confused.

ALANA

I guess.

ANDRE

Chloe said your choreography was miraculous.

ALANA

It felt miraculous while I was doing it, to be honest.

ANDRE

So you have to go back and dwell in that space; that miracle.

ALANA

I'm not used to talking to people like you.

ANDRE

Who are people like me?

ALANA

People who have things to say.

ANDRE

I have a brain, I use it.

ALANA

I spend a lot of time playing games on my phone.

ANDRE

Why do you live in a way that you're secretly ashamed of?

ALANA

Because that's what I want.

ANDRE

That can't be what you want—

ALANA

When I dance, it's like I reverse the catastrophe…play the tape backwards, bring the dead back to life. Or no: it means going even further back, becoming a child again; innocent. She wanted to marry me. I wasn't sure if I was over dating men. And that hurt her. Before she died I was finally at the point where I was willing to say yes. When someone's dead, you remember the essential things. The taste of their mouth, their tone of voice, the way they smelled.

ANDRE

Can I tell you a story?

ALANA

Yes.

ANDRE

When I was a kid, there was an old russian lady who lived in the
apartment on the first floor of the building my family lived in.
She fled Russia during the Great War. I used to visit her every
day after school for me. For years she was my only real friend.
One day I came home and there was an ambulance waiting outside
the building. She was carried out on a stretcher. She never woke
up. I never was able to explain to her that I loved her. That I
had listened to her. That I had heard her story. The names of
little towns in eastern Russia that have long been forgotten. The
names of her grandchildren. Her husbands favorite kind of soup.
Her favorite composers. Her recipes. I learned Russian from her
and I can still speak it...kind of. We have a heaven inside of us:
everything that constitutes memory—

ALANA

I think I need to go be alone.

ANDRE

Understood.

ALANA

Thanks for talking to me.

ANDRE

It was my pleasure. G'night.

ALANA

G'night.

Exit Alana.

SOPHIA

Thank fucking god.

ANDRE

They don't realize how happy they are, diving through clouds of
gravity and grace—

SOPHIA

I'm sure you're gonna complete that thought and it's gonna be
super-duper deep Andre, but can we please not chit-chat? I'm
tired.

ANDRE
  No problem.

SOPHIA
  I'm sorry.

ANDRE
  It's ok.

ANDRE
  I wrote you a check, it's on the fridge.

SOPHIA
  Thanks.

ANDRE
  You're welcome to sleep here tonight, it's late.

SOPHIA
  Thanks. I might. My mom's been kind of a huge cunt lately and
  I'm not sure I feel like going home.

ANDRE
  That's fine.

SOPHIA
  What are you thinking about?

ANDRE
  I thought you didn't want to chit-chat—

SOPHIA
  Well I changed my mind.

ANDRE
  When you're my age, you would give all of your last thirty years
  for one of your first thirty. That's all....I'm gonna go outside and
  smoke a cigarette, would you like to join me?

SOPHIA
  I think I'm just gonna lay down on the couch and close my eyes
  for a bit.

ANDRE
  Fair enough.

    Exit Andre.

ACT II

Sophia dims the lights and lays down on the couch.Dark stage.

The sound of someone fiddling with the front door.

Enter Charlie.

He brings the lights up.

Sophia sits up, groggy.

SOPHIA
  Hi.

CHARLIE
  I don't think we've met.

SOPHIA
  Clearly.

CHARLIE
  I'm—

SOPHIA
  Charlie. The guy who's always late.

CHARLIE
  I have a reputation.

SOPHIA
  I have a headache.

CHARLIE
  Do you have a name?

SOPHIA
  No.

CHARLIE
  Ok.

SOPHIA
  Are you always this bashful?

CHARLIE
  I feel like we've met before.

SOPHIA
Please don't use lines like that on me.

CHARLIE
No, I'm serious—

SOPHIA
We haven't met before.

CHARLIE
Are you sure?

SOPHIA
Yes.

CHARLIE
Because I really feel like we have.

SOPHIA
We assuredly have not.

CHARLIE
You're a memory of the future—aren't you?

SOPHIA
You feel like thoughtful human, which is interesting.

CHARLIE
Do you not meet thoughtful humans on a regular basis?

SOPHIA
No. Which is why I'm intrigued by you.

CHARLIE
I'm intrigued by you too, in case that's unclear. Which I don't imagine it is.

SOPHIA
This is confusing...

CHARLIE
Why is it confusing?

SOPHIA
Because!

CHARLIE
Because what?

SOPHIA
  I'm not used to this.

CHARLIE
  What's this?

SOPHIA
  Someone whose ears have souls inside them.

CHARLIE
  Hmm.

SOPHIA
  What?

CHARLIE
  It's a shame, that's all.

SOPHIA
  What is?

CHARLIE
  So much self-doubt—

SOPHIA
  Is that what you think it is?

CHARLIE
  That's what I know it is.

SOPHIA
  I don't like when people make assumptions about me.

CHARLIE
  But that's what I'm good at—

SOPHIA
  You should be content with only knowing what I tell you.

CHARLIE
  Says who?

SOPHIA
  Says my anxiety.

CHARLIE
  Tell me about that—

SOPHIA
  I'm gonna leave.

CHARLIE
  Stay.

SOPHIA
  Ok bye now.

CHARLIE
  Wait.

SOPHIA
  Why?

CHARLIE
  I don't know, just wait.

SOPHIA
  Ok.

CHARLIE
  Ok.

SOPHIA
  What do you want me to say?

CHARLIE
  You chase the sweetness of spring all the way to the end of
  summer, and by that time, it's gone—

SOPHIA
  Too late for what?

CHARLIE
  Being happy.

SOPHIA
  Are you unhappy?

CHARLIE
  We're not at the end of summer yet.

SOPHIA
  I don't get what you're saying.

CHARLIE
  How many people have you slept with?

SOPHIA
I'm not gonna tell you that! What's wrong with you?

CHARLIE
I'm just curious.

SOPHIA
I'm not gonna fucking tell you dude.

CHARLIE
Fine.

SOPHIA
Two.

CHARLIE
I see.

SOPHIA
You?

CHARLIE
Fifty-six.

SOPHIA
Are you kidding me?

CHARLIE
No.

SOPHIA
That's so weird.

CHARLIE
Why?

SOPHIA
It's just weird.

CHARLIE
If you sleep with a few people every year for your whole adult life, it adds up.

SOPHIA
You're a whore—

CHARLIE
I like to touch and be touched.

SOPHIA
You're a whore—

CHARLIE
Let's change the subject.

SOPHIA
What I like about summer nights is that everything vanishes but space, the stars, the trees...

CHARLIE
You should keep talking—

SOPHIA
I don't like giving words away. They're mine.

CHARLIE
They're a gift—

SOPHIA
I get the feeling that you have enough words to give away without second thought, but I don't, so—

CHARLIE
I think it's the other way around—

SOPHIA
If I open up, people start asking for too much.

CHARLIE
I'm not people—

SOPHIA
Yet, you're already starting to do it....There are scars on my brain. I flashback to parts of childhood I never wanna see again. Things I can't talk about. And won't talk about. I never feel clean waking up next to someone, no matter who they are. The idea of sleeping next to an adult...man...makes me uncomfortable.

CHARLIE
On the drive up, I kept looking out the window and wondering why everything was so overdeveloped, so soulless. Then stretches of real forest or countryside would suddenly appear and I'd feel ok; calm; in the right place. Then more development, more strip-malls, and McMansions, and I'd start to feel depressed...and angry again—

SOPHIA

I wish hearts could dilate, like pupils do when you go the eye-doctor and get those drops—

CHARLIE

Yeah, me too.

SOPHIA

I feel like a flower, closed, brightly folded, dreaming of the future while still inside the seed, at the beginning of spring.

CHARLIE

Is this a dangerous conversation?

SOPHIA

In school I'd always get in trouble for day-dreaming; which I never understood, because I thought education was supposed to be about learning to see what's invisible—

CHARLIE

One of the most uncanny things about Shakespeare, that people always forget, is that he made Juliet fourteen years old...

SOPHIA

OK. I'm going home now.

CHARLIE

Um.

SOPHIA

Don't look so crestfallen.

CHARLIE

I—

SOPHIA

Just don't. I'm not worth it.

CHARLIE

Worth what exactly?

SOPHIA

Don't play dumb.

CHARLIE

I still don't know your name.

SOPHIA

Sophia. I'm Andre's art model.

CHARLIE

Of course you are.

SOPHIA

Oh please—

CHARLIE

What?

SOPHIA

You're too absorbed in your own idealizations right now to see
that you could really hurt me.

CHARLIE

I like sitting at sidewalk cafes and trying to pick out the people
who haven't gone completely dead inside—it's one of my favorite
games—

SOPHIA

Please don't confuse me for someone who's alive inside.

CHARLIE

You've changed everything for me—

SOPHIA

We just met, bud.

CHARLIE

Because now I know I can swim free from the burden of time,
back into this moment—whenever I need it—

SOPHIA

Uhuh.

CHARLIE

Tell me you feel differently—

SOPHIA

I feel differently.

CHARLIE

You're not very convincing.

SOPHIA

I'm gonna go.

CHARLIE

Where?

SOPHIA

Home. I can walk.

CHARLIE

I'll walk with you.

SOPHIA

No that's alright. Thanks. Bye.

Exit Sophia.

Enter Victoria.

VICTORIA

This room feels elegiac....Can you say something?

CHARLIE

No.

VICTORIA

I miss you. I miss you. I keep thinking it but not saying it.

CHARLIE

Uhuh.

VICTORIA

But then again, you have this way of making me feel very small that makes me not have any regrets.

CHARLIE

I'm sorry if I'm being cold.

VICTORIA

You're not being cold, that's not it.

CHARLIE

Explain then—

VICTORIA

You're depriving me of oxygen, not heat. You're not cold, you're suffocating.

CHARLIE
You used to say that I was the oxygen you breath.

VICTORIA
Just let me feel what I feel.

CHARLIE
I don't want to be that person.

VICTORIA
What person?

CHARLIE
The magical one that you imagine I am.

VICTORIA
But you are magical.

CHARLIE
Everybody's magical if they want to be.

VICTORIA
No, just you.

CHARLIE
If you want to direct a play where all the time and the energy is devoted to language, thought-process, emotion—then do it.

VICTORIA
What do you think I've been trying to do?

CHARLIE
You like the sense of control directing gives you—

VICTORIA
You have no right to say things like that.

CHARLIE
Our relationship was a career choice for you.

VICTORIA
Don't ever fucking say something like that again—

CHARLIE
Alright.

VICTORIA

Your mind is always always going going going; absorbing information and turning it into judgments about everything; about everyone—

CHARLIE

I can't help it.

VICTORIA

Can I touch you, later?—if you're sleeping here, I mean. I need to, I need something—

CHARLIE

No.

VICTORIA

Don't look at me like I'm hurting you, I'm not hurting you, I'm just trying to be warm...I mean, I need to know that it's still there—

CHARLIE

It's not.

VICTORIA

Let me at least hold your hand. There's nothing wrong with that.

CHARLIE

Remember: you're the one who left me.

VICTORIA

There was nothing to leave! We would fuck and then you would go off and write and not talk to me.

CHARLIE

Why do you want to touch me then? I don't get it.

VICTORIA

Because we're free to make new kinds of choices—

CHARLIE

Freedom is lost proportional to the amount of time that's passed. We were most free the day we met and we are the least free now, at this moment.

VICTORIA

Do you really think that's true?

CHARLIE

The fact that human beings gave language a future tense is a tragic error.

VICTORIA

What hurt me the most was knowing how easily you fell in love with other women—

CHARLIE

Perseus, when he went to slay the Medusa, was given, by Athena, a resplendent mirror to escape the monster's direct glance, which would have turned him into stone. But the modern Perseus, who has no mirror, must make a mirror with the surface of his own eyes.

VICTORIA

Anything else on your mind?

CHARLIE

In a theater, even if an actor has a heart attack and dies onstage, the audience always interprets it as part of the show.

VICTORIA

You fucker.

CHARLIE

What?

VICTORIA

Don't lecture me about what happens in the theater.

CHARLIE

I have an enormous appetite to see life as I know it presented back to me onstage, but the problem is, I wasted so much time believing that you could give it to me.

VICTORIA

Every single piece of drama you've produced has the same storyline: sophisticated slash enlightened writer becomes romantically involved with a woman, but she is too neurotic slash hysterical to let go of the fears keeping her from being with him, so she chooses a philistine instead, while the enlightened writer makes the noble choice to move on with his life because he knows the TRUTH....But I still I wish you hadn't stopped writing plays for me...

CHARLIE
Yeah, and I wish you hadn't kept your Tindr account open while we were dating.

VICTORIA
You wanted me to.

CHARLIE
What?

VICTORIA
You couldn't handle monogamy—

CHARLIE
That's your projection—

VICTORIA
Whatever, whatever, whatever. I'd just like to know why we had to stop working together. Can you just tell me that?

CHARLIE
No.

VICTORIA
I can't handle all these silent unspoken little games being played out simultaneously, like I'm playing ten games of chess at once.

CHARLIE
All I said was 'no.'

VICTORIA
'No' is a brutal word-game move.

CHARLIE
I can't help how I talk.

VICTORIA
I feel like the art in me is dying. And I feel like that gives you pleasure.

CHARLIE
Art requires moral vigilance. An unerring sense of what really counts in being alive.

VICTORIA
You seem content with being enigmatic and unkind.

CHARLIE

I'm protecting myself.

VICTORIA

From what?

CHARLIE

Interpretation.

VICTORIA

Coward.

CHARLIE

You cut too many lines—

VICTORIA

What?

CHARLIE

You always cut my plays to the bone. You never trusted what was on the page.

VICTORIA

Because you trusted it too much—

CHARLIE

I trusted that even my mistakes would yield insight, but you insisted on a shallow kind of perfection instead—

VICTORIA

Why didn't you stop me?

CHARLIE

Because that would have required having to explain the significance of—

VICTORIA

You have this way of speaking, Charlie, that's poetic and beautiful; but in your plays, it gets really fucking boring.

CHARLIE

The less talented someone is, the more they cling to their convictions.

VICTORIA

You never actually reflect on yourself; you just force other people to do it—

CHARLIE
Self-reflection is trivializing.

VICTORIA
No: it's humanizing.

CHARLIE
I want to be around people who are happiest when they're themselves.

VICTORIA
Are you one of those people?

CHARLIE
I don't have a self to be happy being.

VICTORIA
I miss you.

CHARLIE
I'm sorry.

VICTORIA
You're sorry? You're ruthless—

CHARLIE
Genius means having a special relationship with time: it means seeing the devastation that time produces. So make a play about that. Make a play about lost time. Then you might actually have something.

VICTORIA
All I can think of are metaphors of the —pursuit, footsteps— when I'm in the same room with you.

CHARLIE
You remember me as exciting, but the truth is, you got bored of me, and you'd get bored again.

VICTORIA
I wasn't bored, I was hurt you didn't need me more.

CHARLIE
You never give an atom more care or affection than the other person does. And it's carefully calculated to be that way.

VICTORIA

I'm giving now—

CHARLIE

The second I touched you again, you'd be satisfied and begin to withhold again.

VICTORIA

That's enough—

CHARLIE

Even now, you like that you're getting attention from me.

VICTORIA

Not this kind—

CHARLIE

Precisely this kind. You suspect that it conceals love.

VICTORIA

There's no love here.

CHARLIE

It's so stupid.

VICTORIA

You're tiresome.

CHARLIE

It's one of my better qualities.

VICTORIA

There's a pain so utterly…so utterly, I don't know. There's a pain that swallows up the rest of me, when you're in the room.

CHARLIE

How do you think that makes me feel?—to be the root of someone else's unhappiness?

VICTORIA

It's not something I think about.

CHARLIE

Figures.

VICTORIA

You have a way of making other people feel selfish for not feeding your selfishness.

CHARLIE
Point taken.

VICTORIA
I just feel so powerless.

CHARLIE
I don't know what that means.

VICTORIA
You wouldn't.

CHARLIE
I don't what that means either—

VICTORIA
Life for me is like standing by a fire but not being able to feel any warmth. I keep fueling it; keeping piling on kindling…but I still feel cold—

CHARLIE
Ok—

VICTORIA
Still feel overwhelmingly bitter—

CHARLIE
Ok—

VICTORIA
It's like I have two selves: one which acts confidently and the other which feels mocked by people who have the confidence I secretly lack….Which is why I don't like certain aspect of your work: because what you write makes me feel like I'm being mocked by a superior person….It makes me feel more like myself, but I don't know who that person is. And I keep expecting you to see that, Charlie, but instead, you continue to write plays that make me feel inconsolable and empty. And I think that's actually a flaw in your art, but I don't have the confidence to tell you that; so yeah, I'm passive-aggressive and political and make cuts and interpretations you don't like. Yeah. I do. But the fact is, you never really let me be your equal—

CHARLIE

You convert everything into self-pity: it's the only way you maintain an identity. If you stopped pitying yourself even for a second, you'd cease to know who you are. You'd stumble around as if you'd been blinded—

VICTORIA

I have a question: how do you permit yourself to be so cruel to other people?

CHARLIE

I had a poetry in me near to the world of music…and you never heard it. You didn't want to hear it. Because you were jealous of it. Like you still are.

VICTORIA

I think we should discontinue this conversation.

CHARLIE

Agreed.

Exit Victoria.

Exit Charlie, who turns off the lights on his way out.

Enter Fred, then Chloe.

Fred switches on a light.

CHLOE

Fred: I've got to kiss someone tonight or my self esteem will drop perilously low.

FRED

I'm the wrong person to ask.

CHLOE

You're the worst.

FRED

I'm aware.

CHLOE

Aren't you attracted to me?

FRED

That's not the issue.

CHLOE

Then what is?

FRED

Time.

CHLOE

What are you talking about?

FRED

I still think about the day we met. It was early September.
Sophomore year. You were reading under a tree. Your hair was
longer then, and the wind whipped through it like a knife. And I
stood there, in the middle of campus staring at you and you didn't
notice. It was at that time that you became my passion.

CHLOE

So let me get this straight, because I'm your passion, you won't
kiss me—

FRED

You ignored me that whole year. I'm guessing you don't
remember. You were going out with that guy Sam who gave you
coke whenever you needed it, which was constantly. You only
called me when you needed to cry on the phone to someone. On
countless occasions, I was there for you, and never once did you
thank me. Not one time.

CHLOE

Is it too late to apologize?

FRED

Yes and no.

CHLOE

I don't enjoy the feeling that my emotions are on the line, while
yours are sealed away in a vault somewhere in your icy brain. One
minute I'm looking at you in the moonlight and dammit if I'm not
smitten, and the next minute I'm forced to swallow those feelings
and just accept that you won't accept them—

FRED

It's not that I won't accept them—

CHLOE

Then what is it?

FRED

It's that I can't reciprocate them.

CHLOE

I was 19, Fred—

FRED

I understand that—

CHLOE

Did I really hurt you that much?

FRED

More than you know. More than you'll ever know.

CHLOE

I feel sick to my stomach.

FRED

How do you think I feel?

CHLOE

Do you really think I didn't notice you that first year? Of course
I did, you doofus. I wanted you badly, but I didn't have the
confidence to pursue anything. I still don't.

Fred puts on a record, very softly.

FRED

Somebody told me once the word, fugue, in music, means to flee:
so that Bach's melody lines are like he's running away.

CHLOE

What are you running away from?

FRED

Feeling.

CHLOE

With me?

FRED

Feeling in general.

CHLOE

Your whole personality is a weird mixture of superiority and isolation—

FRED

I'm a hermit crab, living in an abandoned shell.

CHLOE

I think of the men and women I've danced with, the men and women I've kissed. I think of cold nights in high school unzipping, unbuttoning, looking, not touching, or touching and then licking, stroking, probing in the cab of my pickup truck.... and I still have no clue what to do with you—

FRED

I've always thought that what's most beautiful in men is something feminine...and that what's most beautiful in women is something masculine...

CHLOE

I can't tell who is more insecure, you or me—

FRED

Me.

CHLOE

You don't act like it.

FRED

Which is why—

CHLOE

The moonlight is so quiet in the window's darkness. It's just laying there, like an old book. It reminds me of childhood.

FRED

Me too.

CHLOE

What do you want from people Fred?

FRED

Honesty. Something to say and the courage to say it.

CHLOE

It's so rapey, you know? And ultimately so ugly: turning another person on and claiming that you've unlocked some secret. So I'm hungry. So I'm turned on. So what?

FRED

So nothing.

CHLOE

Are you sure?

FRED

Space between people is an indication that they haven't understood what it means to have lived that other person's life.

CHLOE

What don't I understand about you Fred?

FRED

That I'm trying to learn how to bring my beliefs to life, because I can't bring myself to bury them forever.

CHLOE

What are you talking about? What beliefs?

FRED

What I said about seeing you reading under the tree—

CHLOE

I think I'll be able to make it through my 20's without having really risked anything or made a sincere effort at accomplishing anything. I think I've figured it out; how to fool everyone into letting me do that.

FRED

Have you fooled yourself?

CHLOE

You know, I once saw a psychiatrist who said it was a miracle I've survived the world that I built in my head.

FRED

Miracles are the only thing I actually believe in...

CHLOE
Every time I get close to really trusting you, I see this little shift behind your eyes; this little squirming atom of doubt—

FRED
It's not doubt.

CHLOE
What is it?

FRED
I already told you—

CHLOE
But I don't believe it—

FRED
Understanding is there, behind the fear: you have to let your mind move past all its caution, past the behaviors that keep the fear at bay, so that you can know yourself, so that you can know if this is really something you want—

CHLOE
Do you want to know what I think Fred? I think you can't—refuse to—write anything because it would mean competing with Charlie, with your so-called best friend. And not because you're afraid of not measuring up to him as an artist, but because you know that you'd easily surpass him if you tried. It suites you: playing the side-kick. The keyword being playing—acting—which makes you extremely selfish—incredibly selfish—are you listening to me?

FRED
Trying.

CHLOE
Do you feel like you resent women for wanting you to be dominating or aggressive when you can't be, or don't want to be?

FRED
I don't have the level of self-awareness required to answer that question.

CHLOE
I don't idealize you. I just like you.

FRED
But you don't trust me.

CHLOE
No. How could I?

FRED
I find that unforgivable.

CHLOE
I don't like that you can decide to pull the plug whenever you
want so that I'm left wondering what the fuck just happened.
I don't like the total lack of agency I have. You seem like an
emotional person, who wants to open up: but clearly, it's
impossible.

FRED
I've been trying to warn you—

CHLOE
Years of anticipation. It's so disappointing.

FRED
I know.

The sound of thunder.

The sound of a downpour.

Exit Fred.

The rain fades.

The sound of birds.

Warm morning light.

Enter Andre, with a sketch-pad.

*Enter Chloe, who picks up a phone from the coffee-table and begins
to scroll through it.*

Chloe puts the phone down.

CHLOE
The storm last night was beautiful, like a foreign lady in furs and
pearls.

ANDRE
I slept through it.

CHLOE
I think I have a pituitary tumor, I can feel a lump on the back of my head. I need to see a doctor.

ANDRE
Oh kid, please don't do this.

CHLOE
That's all I could think about when I woke up.

ANDRE
What did you have last week?

CHLOE
Last week I was showing severe signs of lupus.

ANDRE
And the week before?

CHLOE
I have an auto-immune disorder!

ANDRE
I'm just saying—

CHLOE
Uncle Andre, if you had endocrines like mine—

ANDRE
A painting shouldn't force an emotion to come through. The emotion should lean back in the darkness of the frame: innocent and supercharged.

CHLOE
I don't think my nervous system can handle moving back to the city.

ANDRE
Then don't—

CHLOE
I'm just so tired of boys who read Kafka on the train—

ANDRE
You mean boys who love to be seen reading Kafka on the train—

CHLOE
But then again, I love waking up with unwashed hair, slept-in clothes, a missing purse, a body that smells like old vegetables next to me.....Uncle Andre—

ANDRE
What?

CHLOE
You weren't asleep last night, I heard you sobbing.

ANDRE
Oops.

CHLOE
I wanna know why.

ANDRE
The divorce blah blah blah.

CHLOE
I saw Aunt Karen a few days ago.

ANDRE
Where?

CHLOE
She was at a coffeeshop downtown somewhere.

ANDRE
Did you say anything to her?

CHLOE
No, I just saw her in the window.

ANDRE
Was she with anyone?

CHLOE
Come on—

ANDRE
Obviously I'd want to know.

CHLOE

She was alone.

ANDRE

Thank you.

CHLOE

I want to move up here for a little while I think.

ANDRE

Your Dad would feel betrayed.

CHLOE

I just want to know if there is any more painful a gift than a compassionate heart—

ANDRE

"The cypresses are always occupying my thoughts," Van Gogh wrote in a letter to his brother Theo, "I should like to make something of them like the canvases of the sunflowers, because it astonishes me that they have not yet been done as I see them."

CHLOE

I think it's just a matter of being able to get my nervous system back up and running so that I can actually feel what I'm experiencing—

ANDRE

Being entirely honest with oneself is a good exercise.

CHLOE

My life is like a gynecologist visit that never ends.

ANDRE

Um.

CHLOE

I spend most of my time looking for excuses for low-level depression.

ANDRE

I've noticed.

CHLOE

Most of the time, with people, I'm just trying to get laid, or trying to explain that I want to get laid, but not with them.

ANDRE
Sucks.

CHLOE
So I'm left fucking the people I hate, and hating the people I want to fuck; and doing the jobs I want to quit and quitting the jobs I want to keep.

ANDRE
Sucks.

CHLOE
I really believe that God shouldn't give us names, as if we're actually individuals: he should just have us numbered, like cattle or baseball cards.

ANDRE
True.

CHLOE
Sometimes, when I'm up here, I go for long walks and I feel like I'm in another world, like the English countryside as Shakespeare knew it, which is weird because I've never been to England, and definitely not four hundred years ago. And it's so emotional. The music of the apple-trees. And the dead parts of me that toss in the wind like laundry on the line—

ANDRE
There are two kinds of people: those who can endure physical pain but not spiritual pain, and those who can endure spiritual pain but go crazy over the thought of physical pain.

CHLOE
Which kind of person are you?

ANDRE
I think it's self-evident.

CHLOE
Most people usually listen to me with pity in their eyes. Except for you Andre—

ANDRE
When I was younger, I painted haunted figures with precarious sanity. As I've got older, I suppose I've learned to smile a little bit more with the paint-brush...

CHLOE

I wish you and my Dad were still on good terms.

ANDRE

Brothers are always fragments of their father. And they resent it. They wish they were whole people. But they're not. They're just aspects of this god-like person who is only vaguely aware of their existence.

CHLOE

Isn't it a pride thing though, at this point? Like you could just pick up the phone—

ANDRE

I think I'm gonna go work in the garden for a little while. It was nice talking to you Chloe.

Exit Andre.

Chloe picks up the guitar and begins to strum.

Enter Leo.

LEO

Morning.

CHLOE

I know you're in the closet Leo.

LEO

Woah...

CHLOE

I know you're not gonna acknowledge it—

LEO

Fuck.

CHLOE

You shouldn't have left your phone out here.

LEO

Fuck.

CHLOE

You don't have to say anything.

LEO
It's happened a few times: with men.

CHLOE
Ok then.

LEO
I haven't told anyone.

CHLOE
You don't have to be embarrassed.

LEO
Of course I don't. That's not the issue.

CHLOE
What is then?

LEO
The issue is that nothing is private—

CHLOE
You're afraid of Dad finding out—

LEO
I'm afraid of a lot of things.

CHLOE
Why can't you make eye-contact?

LEO
I'm gonna go make breakfast. I think I'm gonna make scrambled eggs. Do you want some?

CHLOE
Yeah, that'd be nice.

LEO
Ok. I'll make some then.

Exit Leo.

Chloe walks to the guitar, picks it up, sits down again, and begins to play.

Gradual blackout.

ACT III

A year later.

A summer night.

Cozy, romantic light.

Leo and his new boyfriend Arthur hold hands. Surrounding them are Victoria, Charlie, Fred, and Alana.

Away from the main group, Andre paints Sophia, who is frozen in pose.

ALANA
Did anyone else watch the sunset? It was full of echoes.

ARTHUR
I play this game with my cat called 'love or hungry' where I let the cat follow me around and I try to guess whether she's hungry or loves me. The answer is always 'hungry.'

FRED
How's the new apartment?

VICTORIA
There's room for a bed and a little desk. Charlie writes all day and I read: it's cozy.

CHARLIE
I have a splitting headache.

VICTORIA
Is something wrong?

CHARLIE
No, I just need to go for a little walk.

Exit Charlie.

VICTORIA
He called me out of the blue last winter…or, rather, he called me
for a week until I picked up and he was like, hey, I love you and
I'm writing something new, let's be together again. And I said yes
for some reason. Is that true happiness? Maybe. But it feels more
like the set-up to a really cruel joke.

LEO
I'm really stoked about rehearsals starting next week—

VICTORIA
Do you like the text?

LEO
It's great.

VICTORIA
Yeah…

ALANA
What?

VICTORIA
Creeping ambivalence. Fear that the neurotic energy from my
relationship will spill into my art, contaminate it.

LEO
The play is actually good though—

VICTORIA
It makes me cry when I read it out-loud: even if it doesn't have
a title or a structure or an ending. But, I don't know: I'm still
nervous about it. The whole thing is inexplicable.

ARTHUR
I need a support group for owners of overweight cats—

FRED
Why does the play make you cry?

VICTORIA
Because that's when I get to talk to the person I live with.

FRED
Hmm.

VICTORIA
What are you thinking?

FRED
Words flood out of us. But when the flood subsides, we're left standing in the mud.

ARTHUR
I feel like my Instagram account is my major accomplishment in life.

VICTORIA
Fred—

FRED
I'm not sure what you expect me to say.

VICTORIA
Fred, are you still working on a book?

FRED
I am.

LEO
I tried to write a novel last year, but I wrote like six pages and gave up. I just, like, fucking gave up. I don't like existing on a psychological level, it makes me feel awkward.

ARTHUR
He's so cute.

LEO
I grew up in a household where feelings weren't discussed.

VICTORIA
What was discussed instead?

CHLOE
Grades, sports, music lessons, money.

ANDRE
You have to get over it—

CHLOE
Get over what?

ANDRE
The values that were chosen for you.

LEO
They're embedded in my skin, like shrapnel.

FRED
Then pull the pieces out, one by one.

ARTHUR
I don't know who shows me less affection: Princess or Leo.

VICTORIA
You look uncomfortable.

LEO
I am uncomfortable dude.

ARTHUR
He's different when we're alone.

LEO
Arthur...

ARTHUR
It's true. That's when the queen comes out.

LEO
Arthur...

ARTHUR
When my sister turned twenty-one, I took her to a shitty drag
bar because I think it's important for people to see other people
resisting hegemony—

LEO
I know I'm cut off from myself in, like, significant ways. Ok?

FRED
We all are.

ARTHUR
I feel like my Instagram account is my major accomplishment
in life. I only post pictures of Princess though. No humans. That
would be so rude.

CHLOE
Fred can you not sit so close to me?

FRED
Sorry.

ARTHUR
You hurt his feelings.

CHLOE
He's fine.

ARTHUR
I think he's gonna cry. Why are you giving me that look?

LEO
Because you're being annoying.

ARTHUR
I'm the life of the party.

LEO
You're annoying.

ARTHUR
You're jealous.

CHLOE
Why is the mood in the room so heavy?

ARTHUR
People probably have to take a shit.

CHLOE
Gross.

ARTHUR
Oh do your bodies not contain any fecal matter? I'm sorry, I come
from a planet where shit gets real.

VICTORIA
I'm gonna go talk to Charlie—

ALANA
Don't.

VICTORIA
But I want to.

FRED

Don't.

VICTORIA

Fred please tell me why not?

FRED

Because that's not how this works.

VICTORIA

What's this?

FRED

People.

CHLOE

It makes you feel powerful, doesn't it?—acting like you have some kind of extra-special insight—

FRED

Not necessarily.

CHLOE

It pisses me off. I wish the rest of you would stop asking him questions as if he has answers for things.

ARTHUR

I have answers for things—

CHLOE

I'm sure you do Arthur.

ARTHUR

I'm serious.

CHLOE

Ok.

ARTHUR

I feel like one of those guitars that sounds OK on its own, but is out of tune with everybody else in the band, but doesn't know it's out of tune with the rest of the band.

CHLOE

Fred can you at least get drunk with us tonight?

FRED

  I'll think about it.

CHLOE

  I think that's the only way I can stand being in the same room
  with you.

ALANA

  Dose anyone have a sleeping pill?

ARTHUR

  Sleeping pills fuck up my morning sex with Leo—

LEO

  I want to die—

CHLOE

  I have some, I'll give them to you later—

ARTHUR

  But then again I've always hated morning sex. I think it's my
  least sexy hour. My mouth is dry, my crotch is dry. Like, let me
  get well-oiled and running first. We can all benefit from some
  lubrication...

ALANA

  Arthur, can ask you a question?

ARTHUR

  Go for it—

ALANA

  Who are you?

ARTHUR

  Leo's boyfriend.

ALANA

  Aside from that—

ARTHUR

  I'm the poetic self forgotten by the world of the repressed-as-fuck
  bourgeoisie.

Arthur takes a bag of weed from his pocket and hands it to Leo.

ARTHUR

Can you roll that for me? My hands are occupied.

LEO

With what?

ARTHUR

Mental masturbation.

LEO

Whatever.

Leo begins to roll the joint.

ALANA

I haven't done anything creative for a year.

CHLOE

I think I'm gonna move to LA.

ARTHUR

I usually don't tweet my real thoughts, but I'll share this one: I'm guessing that none of you grew up poor.

LEO

No, we didn't.

ALANA

I've developed a morbid heart—and I can't bring myself to discuss the reason why.

ARTHUR

You're the girl whose girlfriend died right?

ALANA

Yeah.

ARTHUR

See, it's easy to talk about it.

ALANA

It's actually a relief to hear someone name it.

ARTHUR

See—

ALANA

I keep waiting for a memory to form, like the bloom in the flower, but it doesn't. The inside of my skull remains murky, vague, cold.

CHLOE

Tonight is kinda horrible.

ALANA

I often think: shouldn't we be celebrating life? Why do we insist on burying it?

ARTHUR

Leo, you have to roll that joint faster—

CHLOE

I'm becoming increasingly conscious of how claustrophobic our social circle is.

ARTHUR

I've been trying to tell ya'll...

FRED

Can you define claustrophobic for us?

CHLOE

A place where suffering can't escape itself.

ALANA

Why don't we go for a walk?

CHLOE

Alright. I'd prefer to get high though, first.

Leo lights the joint, takes a hit, and passes it to Chloe.

Chloe takes a couple hits and stands up and hands the joint to Fred, who inhales.

CHLOE

Ok, let's go.

Fred hands the joint to Vitoria. Victoria shakes her head and passes the joint on.

VICTORIA

I'm trying to give up smoking—

ARTHUR
Oh hell no—

VICTORIA
It makes my insomnia worse.

ARTHUR
When I can't sleep, I talk to Pan.

VICTORIA
Pan, like the The God of Nature?

ARTHUR
Precisely. You see: Pan is buried deep in mythic time, like a pearl at the bottom of the ocean. Which is why he wants people to talk to him: because he's all alone.

FRED
What do you and Pan talk about?

ARTHUR
Well, Pan DOES talk A LOT about himself. But it's ok, because he's fabulous.

VICTORIA
Can I meet Pan?

ARTHUR
I wouldn't get your hopes up.

VICTORIA
Why not?

ATHUR

Because you're still heavily brain-washed by the world-wide, totalitarian conspiracy of money.

VICTORIA
That's news to me...

ARTHUR
Princess introduced me to Pan. I love her so much.

LEO
He literally talks to the cat all day. I'm not kidding.

ARTHUR

Bitch is just jealous. Pan once told me: 'Arthur, you could recite the name of for love in all the languages of the world, but at the end of your life, you still wouldn't know what love was if you hadn't experienced it for yourself.' Isn't that deep? Andre—tell me it's deep—

ANDRE

It's deep.

ARTHUR

Because, in my life, I never really had anybody to love; nobody who'd cry if I died—because God knows Leo is too withholding to shed a tear.

VICTORIA

I still think I need to go talk to Charlie.

FRED

Victoria, I'm telling you...

ARTHUR

Oh my god, I just had a terrible premonition that there's going to be a sudden outbreak of limp dicks in this house tonight: there's too much tension.

LEO

Oh fuck me.

ARTHUR

But don't worry everyone. I spent this afternoon gathering powerful herbs for my patented 'dong-tea.' Want to know the recipe? I don't mind sharing. It's ragweed, peppermint, tabasco sauce, a few moldy peaches, cough syrup, sage, tulips, mint, aspirin, catnip, old newspapers, and mostly importantly—viagra. It's especially helpful for morbid intellectuals. I can make it extra strong for you Fred; though you'd think viagra was the key ingredient, it's really all about the tabasco sauce. Not that I've ever tried some—because God knows my lever doesn't need any extra pushing—but from what Leo tells me—

LEO

Please please please stop talking just long enough for me to recover my dignity...

VICTORIA

We allow so few genuine silences to develop...

FRED

Kill everything to kill the silence.

VICTORIA

A play happens one word at a time, over and over. You can hear the
future coming, like a train in the distance. I like rehearsals because
they end when the future arrives, without consequences....He
sleeps with all the lights on, Charlie. And that's how he fucks me
too. He didn't used to be like that—

ARTHUR

I never told you this Leo, but my father died when I was sixteen.
Hit by a car. No wait, it was a heart attack. No wait, spontaneous
combustion. No wait: it doesn't matter, does it?—a death is a death
is a death. A rose is a rose is a rose. No wait: he shot himself in the
head.

VICTORIA

Jesus...

ARTHUR

What I'm saying is: ya'll need to look for the crease between real
and unreal, true and false. Find where the light seeps in. I'm talking
about here, in America: in this shit, left-for-dead place. In this civil
fucking society. Light. Divine light.

VICTORIA

I wouldn't mind throwing my phone away, moving to a place like
this. Among the wildflowers. Meditatively. I'm not kidding. I
taught an undergraduate drama class this past spring, and I wanted
to stop and shout: run, get out of here, lose your ambition, become
humble, live like a peasant. But I didn't.

ARTHUR

In high school one time, I once got like, super drunk with the
captain of the football team—and blew him in the parking lot of a
grocery store. We never talked about it. He never talked about it. I
think he's married. No, I lied: I know he's married. But I know he
still thinks about it: that sloppy, old BJ; shameless and quick and
perfect as fuck....Princess is probably really upset that I left her
alone for the weekend. She must be so lonely—

LEO

Can you please shut up for a second about the goddamn cat?

ARTHUR

You know Leo, sometimes when you don't sleep over, I go and take a shower with all the lights off so that it's pitch dark; and I finger myself; think about you. Feel you inside me—and the I cum and dry off and fall asleep. Every time you're not there. Every time.

LEO

I feel out of control.

ARTHUR

Good.

LEO

I wish it didn't feel obscene; my desire for you—I wish I could accept it. I wish I could stop pushing you away.

Andre puts down the brush and steps back from the painting.

SOPHIA

My back hurts.

ANDRE

Just give me thirty seconds.

Arthur stands up.

ARTHUR

I need to go smoke in the apple-orchard and visualize for a little while. Go look at my ancestors: the ones who died three thousand billion years ago so that we could have their light at night.

ANDRE

The bugs are gonna eat you alive.

ARTHUR

Better than being eaten alive in here.

Arthur kisses Leo.

ARTHUR

I'm teasing. Love ya. Bye everyone.

Exit Arthur.

LEO
  I need to go talk to him.

  Exit Leo.

VICTORIA
  I wish we were better friends Fred—

FRED
  Doesn't do much good to wish for it.

VICTORIA
  I'm never been sure what to say to you.

ANDRE
  Ok, Sophia we're done. Good work.

Sophie gets up and takes a sweater from a peg on the wall and lays
  down.

FRED
  You don't have to say anything and still be able to communicate.

VICTORIA
  I don't know how to do that.

FRED
  As a director, you should.

Andre puts on a record: the adagio from Mozart's Clarinet Concerto
  in A.

VICTORIA
  I really cannot stand another condescending lecture on my work
  from a man.

  Enter Charlie.

CHARLIE
  Hey guys.

ANDRE
  Hey Charlie.

VICTORIA
  How's your head-ache?

CHARLIE
  You know, piercing.

VICTORIA
Can we go to bed, I'm tired?

Victoria gets up to leave.

CHARLIE
I'll be right up.

VICTORIA
You don't want to come with me?

CHARLIE
I'll be up in five minutes. I wanna talk to Andre for a little while.

VICTORIA
Um. Ok. Well. Then, yeah. Ok. I'll see you soon in that case. G'night everybody.

Exit Victoria.

Andre sits down.

ANDRE
That melody is everything. Everything. Unbearable. When I hear it, images start to flash in mind like the Perseids in the sky.

Every summer near dawn you can see them. The Perseids. In a few hours, they'll flash over the house; a river of dust; a river of light.

Do you hear the clarinet snaking through the strings? It's trying to tell us us how to live with ourselves. How to live with the knowledge that we aren't going to stick around to be remembered; that we're all in the process of disappearing forever.

Which is why Mozart had to write the clarinet concerto: as forgiveness. Forgiveness for being human, finite.

It's like a hand on the forehead.

CHARLIE
There's no way to properly express the feeling that we've gone blind to a whole universe of colors, deaf to the music of wonder.

FRED
There's painting...

CHARLIE

More and more I listen to my friends talk and think: that's the internet expressing itself through you, that's the sound of the system that's eaten you passing you out as gas.

SOPHIA

Andre, you're right about the music—

ANDRE

Of course I am.

CHARLIE

I feel like the rest of our lives is bending around the center of this moment, like light.

SOPHIA

I can feel it too.

ANDRE

I'm going to bed. Have fun kids. Lock up behind you.

Exit Andre.

FRED

I'm clearly not meant to stick around...

CHARLIE

Goodnight Fred. We're due for a talk.

FRED

Maybe tomorrow morning.

CHARLIE

Sounds good.

FRED

Goodnight.

Exit Fred.

SOPHIA

If you stare at someone long enough, they'll eventually look back at you.

CHARLIE

I'm gonna keep looking out the window.

SOPHIA
Why did you write me that letter?

CHARLIE
Why did you never write back?

SOPHIA
I thought it was rude.

CHARLIE
How was it rude?

SOPHIA
You had no right to demand full access to my emotional life.

CHARLIE
Forgive me.

SOPHIA
And you had no right to be so romantic.

CHARLIE
But that's what this is—that's what we are.

SOPHIA
We spent ten minutes together Charlie.

CHARLIE
Which is what makes it so romantic.

SOPHIA
Don't fuck with me.

CHARLIE
I'm not fucking with you.

SOPHIA
It feels like it.

CHARLIE
That's not my intention.

SOPHIA
It's unkind to be so cavalier.

CHARLIE
I didn't know that writing I love you—

SOPHIA

It's insane—

CHARLIE

It's the sanest thing—

SOPHIA

Why do you keep inviting me to your plays?

CHARLIE

Because I keep hoping you'll come.

SOPHIA

We're not friends.

CHARLIE

You knew I'd be here tonight—

SOPHIA

This is my job—

CHARLIE

Oh come on—

SOPHIA

What do you expect me to say? That I was looking forward to seeing you? That I've been nervous about it all week? Yeah. Ok. It's true. I'm glad to see your face. It makes me happy even if it also makes me furious.

CHARLIE

I should have driven up here a year ago and thrown rocks at your window or something—

SOPHIA

It wouldn't have made a difference—

CHARLIE

I don't see why not—

SOPHIA

You're with someone.

CHARLIE

Only because you didn't write me back—

SOPHIA
Please don't say that.

CHARLIE
Please acknowledge—

SOPHIA
Acknowledge what?—that you've formed an unhealthy, irrational attachment to some idealized image of me—sure—I can acknowledge it—can you?

CHARLIE
I'd break my heart for your sake, break it so that you didn't have to break yours.

SOPHIA
I know.

CHARLIE
I saw you right away. And I thought you saw me too.

SOPHIA
Still romantic. Still crazy.

CHARLIE
It was like being in an electrical storm.

SOPHIA
It was ten minutes on an ordinary rainy night when I was 19 years old and we didn't even touch.

CHARLIE
It wasn't ordinary.

SOPHIA
What's your point?

CHARLIE
I don't have one Sophia.

SOPHIA
So why are you still here?

CHARLIE
Out of sheer gratitude.

SOPHIA

Intimacy is so frightening to me.

CHARLIE

It doesn't have to be.

SOPHIA

You're like, sensitive-guy porn.

CHARLIE

I'm not sure what to say.

SOPHIA

Listen: I hugely dislike that I used to abuse myself with alcohol and drugs; sometimes I wonder if that's why I feel this way—whatever way this is—but dwelling on that makes it significantly worse. I think I'm probably a burnout. Or I was at 16 and since then I've been sober and doing yoga five hours a day is actually incredibly boring, but is healthier than trying to slowly kill yourself. A lot has changed for me: food, sleeping pattern, general routine, people. I don't feel very in control, even though I act as if I'm in control. I still live with my Mom, as you may know. I don't sleep well; but when I do, I have very vivid dreams, so vivid I often find it hard to differentiate between the dream and real stuff—

CHARLIE

Sophia—

SOPHIA

Sometimes things don't even seem real. It's more anxiety than depression; it's slowly eating away at my capacity for wonder and that scares me.

CHARLIE

Why are you telling me this?

SOPHIA

So you stop loving me.

CHARLIE

It's just there. The love. Standing in its own light.

SOPHIA

You're gonna make me cry.

CHARLIE
  Look at me—

SOPHIA
  I like to keep the eyes of the soul closed.

CHARLIE
  Sophia, just look at me—

SOPHIA
  Sometimes, when my insomnia is particularly bad, I can't think of
  anything but spending my nights with you; warm and silvery.

CHARLIE
  It kills me to hear you say things like that...

SOPHIA
  I'm sorry.

CHARLIE
  I don't need you to say that you're sorry—

SOPHIA
  You'd spend a day with me and realize you'd made a mistake.

CHARLIE
  You don't know that.

SOPHIA
  Or maybe I'd spend a day with you and realize I'd made the
  mistake.

CHARLIE
  You don't know that either.

SOPHIA
  I'm obsessed with collarbones.

CHARLIE
  What else?

SOPHIA
  The backs of necks too, especially when hair just so delicately
  graces the upper back.

CHARLIE
  What else?

SOPHIA
Extremely quiet, intimate moments with another person.

SOPHIA
Why are we talking about this?

CHARLIE
Because we can.

SOPHIA
I don't trust it—

CHARLIE
I'm not asking you to trust it—

SOPHIA
What are you for asking then?

CHARLIE
To let me trust you.

SOPHIA
I want to trust you too.

CHARLIE
Does that make you uncomfortable?

SOPHIA
Yes.

CHARLIE
Does that make you resent me?

SOPHIA
I'm not sure.

CHARLIE
I wouldn't blame you if it did.

SOPHIA
What a relief.

CHARLIE
I'm sorry.

SOPHIA
Charlie: I'm considering letting you kiss me. Ok?

Charlie moves forward.

SOPHIA
I said considering—

Charlie takes a step back.

CHARLIE
I have as much love in me as blood, so make even the slightest cut and—

SOPHIA
When you inevitably put this moment into a play, don't make me a cartoon. I'm a person, I wanna stay a person.

CHARLIE
You inspire me—

SOPHIA
Which means that I'm just an object—

CHARLIE
No that's not—

SOPHIA
Which means you've already started the process of re-creating who I am—

CHARLIE
Sophia...

SOPHIA
I realized very early on in life that, because I'm beautiful, I'll never have the chance to be anything else. I exist in relation to the body that wants to possess my body. I am invisible until someone sees me. Silent until I'm heard.

CHARLIE
I don't want to defend myself...I don't need to be right—about anything...I just want to be in this room for a little while longer. Ok?—

SOPHIA
The house is so quiet.

CHARLIE
Because I'm asking for mercy—

SOPHIA

I can still feel your vanity, your fear; I can still feel the violence hidden in the way you need me. No matter how far away you are, physically, Charlie.

CHARLIE

Please.

SOPHIA

Reason on the right. Faith on the left. Love right down the middle. And I don't know which way to go.

Enter Victoria.

VICTORIA

Oh, hello.

SOPHIA

Hi—

VICTORIA

Hi Sophia.

VICTORIA

Are you coming to bed?

SOPHIA

I'm going home. Goodnight.

Exit Sophia.

Charlie lets out a deep breath.

VICTORIA

Why was that so awkward?

CHARLIE

You tell me.

VICTORIA

Your eyes are like a funeral Charlie—

CHARLIE

The mysterious thing about spiritual intensity is that it goes dead in the same moment it's born.

VICTORIA
I love you.

CHARLIE
I love you too.

Silence.

Charlie opens his mouth as if to speak and then shuts it.

Charlie leaves, Victoria follows.

Moonlight falls across the floor.

Enter Alana and Chloe

Alana kisses Chloe.

ALANA
I really like you.

CHLOE
Oh.

ALANA
But I'm not sure I'm attracted to people who only gain courage through drinking.

CHLOE
You must not be attracted to many people then.

ALANA
No, I'm not.

CHLOE
I'm obsessed by the idea of feeling the sweat on your skin.

ALANA
It's nice to be touched.

CHLOE
Let's go out in the dark.

ALANA
Aren't Leo and Arthur out there?

CHLOE
The dark is a big place.

ALANA
Not right now.

CHLOE
Why not?

ALANA
Catherine.

CHLOE
I can't compete with a dead woman.

ALANA
I'm sorry.

CHLOE
It was almost two years ago—

ALANA
What are you saying exactly?

CHLOE
Don't listen to me.

ALANA
No: I heard something I didn't want to hear and I now can't unhear it.

CHLOE
I'm being stupid.

ALANA
Yes you are.

CHLOE
Let's just have fun, I'm not trying to make this a big deal.

ALANA
Why can't you see how emotional I am right now?

CHLOE
Probably because I only see what I want to see.

ALANA
Girls starved and desperate for affection refuse to acknowledge the difference between a good and a bad touch...because they're afraid that only accepting the good touch would mean never being touched at all—

84

CHLOE
Yours isn't a bad touch—

ALANA
I'm not touching you, when I touch you, Chloe.

CHLOE
Oh no Alana: you can't say things like that.

ALANA
I'm sorry, but it's true.

CHLOE
But you can't say it, you can't say—not like that. It's not fair. It's too painful. You have to keep certain things to yourself.

ALANA
And I do Chloe. Every day, I mourn in private. Mourn as a sacrifice to a memory that I can't let die…because that would mean letting her die twice…

CHLOE
That has nothing to do with me; nothing to do with right now.

ALANA
Instead of talking to me, you should have just put your hand over my mouth and fucked me against the wall. But you started talking and I started thinking and now I just feel inconsolable.…It's funny, the worst part about grief is how horny it makes you. It's ridiculous.

CHLOE
This is really confusing. You're really confusing.

ALANA
No, it's not. We're friends. We've always been friends. This is just—I dunno—

CHLOE
I think I like being hurt. I think I expect it.

ALANA
I like the feeling of your skin on mine, and I'm sorry if I go carried away.

CHLOE

I have mosquito bites on my ankles, I've been wearing the same dress for two days. I feel a little dehydrated. But I still want the hovering radiance of your fingers to pierce me, make my legs buckle.

ALANA

Do you remember that huge storm last summer?

CHLOE

Yeah.

ALANA

How it woke me up and I saw you standing in the doorway to my bedroom?—

CHLOE

Yeah.

ALANA

What were you doing before you crawled into bed with me?—I never asked.

CHLOE

I was talking to Fred.

ALANA

That's what I thought.

CHLOE

What's your point?

ALANA

Never mind.

CHLOE

What?

ALANA

I like talking to you better when you're sober.

CHLOE

You know, you make people feel like they're on a surgery bed without anesthesia…it's like being first paralyzed and then slowly being cut into, cut apart, broken down…dissected. It's not pleasant.

ALANA

I can't imagine.

CHLOE

Boredom, vanity, shame, fear—these things live inside of me.
They're seeds, sprouting up.

ALANA

I asked about Fred because I'm a jealous person. It kills me to
know that somewhere, you harbor unrequited feelings for him—

CHLOE

It's so hypocritical of you to love, to worship, a dead women and
at the same time, to blame me for the vague, residual feelings I
have for Fred—

ALANA

I know. That's what I've been trying to tell you.

CHLOE

I'm glad I have my brother because that means there's at least one
person who understands—

ALANA

Understands what?

CHLOE

Growing up unloved by the people who made you.

ALANA

Last night, after we drove up, I went for a run along the road
that wraps around the pond. The air smelled warm and heavy,
like someone had just done laundry. I ran for close to two hours
until I felt dehydrated, and when I made it back the porch I just
laid down and cried for another hour…and then I came inside
and had like six glasses of water. Laying down in that warm
laundry summer air, and crying…it goes against the way we've
been trained to think. It's too unproductive, too inefficient,
too emotional….But life is emotional. Death is emotional.
Everything is emotional. And emotions take time.

CHLOE

I'm tired.

ALANA

Do you mind if I sleep in your bed? Maybe it'd be nice if we just cuddled.

CHLOE

No, I don't think I want that.

ALANA

Oh. Ok.

CHLOE

I'm tired of having to beg for affection. It's not doing me any good.

ALANA

I understand.

CHLOE

I'm glad.

ALANA

I love watching the moonlight loop through the window...

CHLOE

Me too.

ALANA

It's like the way a dream looks, splashed along the walls of the skull.

ALANA

It's nice, isn't it?

Gradual blackout.

ACT IV

Unreal light.

Andre enters, sets flowers on the table, steps back, admires them, and then stands before the easel and begins to paint: slowly and meditatively.

Alana is asleep on the couch. She is wearing a warm, autumnal sweater.

ALANA

God, the mornings are really getting cold—

ANDRE

Hello Alana.

ALANA

Hi Andre.

ALANA

I was in the middle of a dream in which you were dead and we were all at your funeral—

ANDRE

Hmm. That's funny.

ALANA

I don't see why—

ANDRE

There are two ways of imagining time. One is as a straight line. The other is a circle. According to the first model, salvation is something we aim towards, like an arrow. According to the second model, which is much older, salvation is something that comes and goes. Winter to spring, summer to fall, fall back to winter, silence, snow.

ALANA

It was extremely upsetting, the dream—

ANDRE

If there's no room to dream, then there's no room to live.

ALANA

I was awarded a really big grant this week, to choreograph my next piece—

ANDRE

Congratulations on the institutionalization of your art.

ALANA

That's what it is…isn't? It's so embarrassing.

ANDRE

No, it's just money. Enjoy it. It doesn't last.

ALANA

I'm really worried about the whole thing—

ANDRE

Because you don't feel like you have anything new to say and the expectations are out of control—

ALANA

Yes.

ANDRE

And you're silently panicking about your capacity to produce authentic work in this new context, so you're hoping that I'll say something that will help illuminate things for you—

ALANA

Yes.

ANDRE

Welp, you're out of luck in that case.

ALANA

Oh.

ANDRE

What do you expect me to say Alana? That it's easy? That failure isn't a possibility? Of course it's a possibility.

ALANA

So what do I do?

ANDRE

If need be, fail, and move on with your life.

ALANA

I don't know where beauty went. I used to see it everywhere.

ANDRE

Beauty resides in a thousand secret harmonies which should be
injected straight into the imagination like a shot of adrenaline—

ALANA

I still play a lot of games on my phone.

ANDRE

Well, you should stop—

ALANA

I can't.

ANDRE

Then don't ask me to help you.

ALANA

I'm sorry if I'm making you angry.

ANDRE

I'm not angry.

ALANA

Are you sure?

ANDRE

Accuracy of the eye, sureness of the hand, the mixing of color,
demands attention at every moment, and the practice of a
lifetime. Aside from the brain, the hands receive more blood
from the heart than any other part of the body. Which means that
the brain and the hands are intimately connected: they wake up
and fall asleep together. When the brain has a nightmare, it's the
hands that wake up coated with sweat.

Andre moves to exit.

ALANA

Where are you going?

ANDRE

I'm going to wake you up.

ALANA

What?

ANDRE

"For my part I know nothing with any certainty, but the sight of the stars makes me dream," Van Gogh said.

ALANA

I don't understand.

ANDRE

Open your eyes—

Exit Andre.

Crisp morning light.

Enter Fred, in jogging clothes, from outside.

Alana rubs her eyes:

ALANA

I was in the middle of a really intense dream—

FRED

Which was what?

ALANA

I was talking to Andre as if he were still alive.

FRED

What did he say?

ALANA

A lot of things.

FRED

It makes sense that you would see him.

ALANA

Why?

FRED

Because you already spend every day with death.

ALANA

Yeah I guess.

FRED

Andre saw the eternal value in turning life into art, and then turning it back again. Back into life. It's the movement that's key: in one direction, with one eye, his paintings appear to be tragedies; with the other, as glory.

ALANA

Fred: I want to cry.

FRED

Then you should cry.

ALANA

But it's something I've been avoiding doing for a really long time...

FRED

That's all the more reason—

ALANA

I need to go—

FRED

I wrote Andre a letter after he died. I found myself writing in a delicate, searching, transparent language. The language I've always wanted to write in, but never could. And I think what I realized, writing that letter, was something I've always instinctively known, but have been afraid to say: that we're saved not by God, but by love. That love is the most we can hope for.

ALANA

I'm going now—

Exit Alana.

Fred sits down.

The light increases, marking the increase of the morning sun.

Charlie enters with a cup of coffee.

FRED

Hey.

CHARLIE

Yo.

FRED

We don't have much to say to each other anymore.

CHARLIE

It's wretched.

FRED

Let's be honest: it's a pride thing.

CHARLIE

Whose pride though?

FRED

Both of ours.

CHARLIE

I don't get it.

FRED

You don't need to.

CHARLIE

I trust you and want you to challenge—

FRED

No you don't.

CHARLIE

Because you hate me.

FRED

Why do you say that?

CHARLIE

I feel it.

FRED

Our words don't have the same freedom anymore.

CHARLIE

I guess not.

FRED

You're more like my brother Charlie, than my friend. And that's really a kind of a miracle—

CHARLIE

I dunno—seems like a cop out to say that—

FRED

I'm not asking you to agree with me.

CHARLIE

You quietly lash out at anyone who asks you to operate on something other than an abstract, symbolic level...

FRED

I already told you that I don't hate you.

CHARLIE

You use all—and I mean all—of your intellectual ability, Fred, to create separation between you and the people around you—

FRED

You want me to say the word 'hate' first, so that you don't have to feel guilty when you say it.

CHARLIE

You're right.

FRED

You're burned out at 27, and I'm just starting—as an artist.

CHARLIE

I know, and I'm trying to forgive you for that.

FRED

Except it's not actually true—

CHARLIE

Don't bullshit me—

FRED

Charlie: that new play you sent me is the best thing you've ever written.

CHARLIE

See, that sounds like bullshit...

FRED

It's not, it's not...your play's a secret love letter...every word of it. After I finished reading it, all I could do was walk around the block and cry.

CHARLIE

It's a mess.

FRED

No, it's exactly what it needs to be.

CHARLIE

It's a mess.

FRED

For the first time, you were able to go beyond yourself and simply write from that invisible place that we all conceal within us: the place in our hearts where love is buried and mourned.

CHARLIE

I'm a mess.

FRED

Right, and I guess you imagine that no one understands the fact that the play is about Sophia and not the person you married. And they probably don't. But I do Charlie. Your brother—I saw it. I saw what happened when you were in the same room with her. And I saw how it changed your work.

CHARLIE

All it did was fuck me up.

FRED

Remember: the artist only has one truth, that love exists. Which is the power of what you've written: it's your waking-up moment—

CHARLIE

Coffee is my waking up moment—

FRED

It's the same the transformation Hamlet undergoes in between Acts 4 and 5 of his play…it's the transformation from a personal vision of life, to an eternal one—

CHARLIE

Hamlet dies at the end of Act 5, Fred, and so does everyone else.

FRED

Shakespeare's the ultimate realist.

CHARLIE

Well, I'm glad you like the new play…I think I needed to hear that it was alright.

FRED

It's more than alright Charlie.

CHARLIE

So yeah. Anyway—

FRED

I've been thinking a lot about the last summer Andre was alive... about my coldness and aloofness towards you and everyone else— and I'm sorry for that. I really am.

CHARLIE

I accept your apology.

FRED

For years, I've been discovering what I am at heart, and only recently have I discovered that I might actually be good. Good at heart. Which means that for first time, I'm able to see how much of my past behavior was really just a projection of my own self-hatred and disgust—

CHARLIE

Now, if only the rest of us could come to the same realization, things might actually be ok around here—

FRED

But this is the point I'm trying to make to you Chuck: you've been given an almost inconceivable gift: the ability to love someone more than you love yourself, and the poetry to express it. So you've got to get rid of the self-pity I see in your eyes: it's not worthy of the miracle that's living inside of you.

CHARLIE

I'm not ready to hear this.

FRED

You need to be.

Enter Victoria, with a pregnant belly.

VICTORIA

Good morning everyone.

FRED

Good morning Victoria. I'm gonna go take a shower—

Exit Fred.

VICTORIA

All the light and fire's gone out of this house.

CHARLIE

I don't know if it was ever there to begin with.

VICTORIA

Charlie, what's wrong?

CHARLIE

Nothing.

VICTORIA

We're having a kid, and I don't even know you—and I don't think that you know me either.

CHARLIE

You're just realizing this now?

VICTORIA

I'm pregnant with a stranger's baby. It's like I've been raped.

CHARLIE

Don't be dramatic.

VICTORIA

Don't be cruel.

CHARLIE

I don't know what you want me to say.

VICTORIA

My parents were such cold people. They barely spoke at dinner. Barely spoke on family vacations. We'd drive for hours. Hours is total silence. That's why I became a director, I think: I had to create characters and then move them around in my head; I had to make sure my imagination put on a good show—otherwise I'd be forced to look at what was going on around me, in the physical world.

Enter Chloe.

The light brightens slightly.

CHLOE

It's such a gorgeous morning. I love the fall...I feel like I'm interrupting something—

VICTORIA
No, it's ok Chloe. Have a seat. It's your house.

CHLOE
Are you sure?

VICTORIA
Seriously, it's fine.

CHLOE
I can make breakfast if anyone's hungry—

VICTORIA
I have morning sickness.

CHARLIE
And I'm not hungry.

CHLOE
Alrighty.

VICTORIA
Is it strange living here by yourself?

CHLOE
Leo and Arthur are here a lot.

VICTORIA
But it's still mostly you—

CHLOE
Yeah.

VICTORIA
It's amazing how much has changed...

CHLOE
A few weeks before Andre went into hospice care, I took the train up to see him. It was around Christmas time. It was snowing. I got to Grand Central early, so I just wondered around, looking up at the artificial stars. That was the moment when the voice in my head that would criticize everything that came out of my mouth finally began to go away. Andre noticed as soon as I got here. I'll never forget what he said: 'In the language of nature, every word is a word for soul.'

VICTORIA

I'll never forget getting that phone call from you saying he had a brain tumor...

CHLOE

I wish he was here for the baby.

VICTORIA

Oh, this makes me sad...

CHLOE

We can change the subject; I think we should.

Enter Arthur.

ARTHUR

Don't worry, I'm here to talk about myself. Where should I start? Oh, I know. Last weekend, I was out for a Sunday night drink by myself because Leo and I were fighting and there were three girls next to me all dolled up and drinking espresso martinis and champagne, so I assumed it was a birthday, but they said, 'No, it's just Sunday, we're going dancing now!' and I was like, 'can I come?' and they were like, 'sure' and it was so much fun.

VICTORIA

I feel bloated.

CHLOE

You're beautiful.

VICTORIA

I'm a balloon.

ARTHUR

I'm so afraid of getting pregnant.

VICTORIA

I don't think you have much to be worried about.

CHLOE

Where's Leo?

ARTHUR

Mr. Grumps is in bed, he'll be down shortly.

CHLOE

Did you talk to Pan last night Arthur?

ARTHUR
Oh hell yeah: Pan had A LOT on his mind.

CHLOE
Like what?

ARTHUR
I can't tell you. It was a private conversation.

CHLOE
That's too bad.

Enter Leo.

ARTHUR
Oh Mr. Grumps is up!

LEO
Morning.

Leo sits down at the table.

LEO
Does anyone want anything, if I drive to town later?

VICTORIA
Can you buy me a quart of ice-cream?

ARTHUR
Lol.

LEO
Yes.

VICTORIA
I can give you cash for it.

LEO
That works.

ARTHUR
Sometimes I'm convinced that I'm either the Buddha or the devil.
I must be one or the other.

Enter Fred, carrying a notebook. He has wet hair.

FRED
The devil.

ARTHUR

You know Leo, what you think you are, you become; that's what the Buddha says. The Buddha who might be me.

CHLOE

I'm gonna go make more coffee, I assume people want some.

Exit Chloe.

ARTHUR

The Buddha says: there are only two mistakes one can make along the road to truth; not going all the way, and not starting. The devil says: you have to let your desires fall asleep, so that they can start to dream again. I think I'd rather be the devil.

VICTORIA

What are you writing Fred?

FRED

It's nothing.

ARTHUR

Mr. Grumps doesn't feel like saying much this morning, does he?

LEO

Arthur, can you please let me sit here and drink my coffee in peace?

ARTHUR

"Please" is such an erotic phrase. "Please do this please." "Please do that." "Please" is the hand which pushes the head down for a blow-job. "Please" gets whispered in the ear; moaned shouted from above. "Please" is a divine phrase.

LEO

Please leave me alone.

ARTHUR

You know, I've been told I can talk snails into orgasm.

LEO

Stop—

ARTHUR

I can't, someone cut the breaks.

Chloe returns with a coffee tray.

ARTHUR

Sometimes I watch you do pushups on the floor of your apartment and I have no idea what your feeling or why your doing pushups. And then I look over, and there's Princess, grooming herself, and I think: I must have a type.

LEO

I never thought I would be able to empathize with Princess, but here I am folks.

VICTORIA

Charlie, can we go upstairs and talk?

CHARLIE

No.

VICTORIA

No?

CHARLIE

Not right now.

VICTORIA

Give me one reason I cannot talk to my husband in private.

CHARLIE

It's the disease talking. The virus of self-awareness that gnaws at my vitals. How comes no one notices that I can barely stand to be in the same room as other human beings?

ARTHUR

I notice—

CHARLIE

Even at the wedding reception, I kept going out for fresh air; inflamed with self-pity....

VICTORIA

Do you realize how painful it is for me to hear you say that in front of everyone? How painful it is for me to hear you say that at all...

CHARLIE

The kinder and more humane a writer is in life, the more merciless they become in their work. The problem is, I've become merciless in life and kind in my work.

VICTORIA

Would everyone else mind giving us a few minutes by ourselves?

CHLOE

Sure, but...

CHARLIE

No one move.

ARTHUR

Oh this is so exciting!

CHARLIE

Autumn used to mean so much to me. Just a few years ago: the first frost or the sight of the leaves turning into rust would give me such a profound sense of clarity. But now all I can feel is the chill in the air....Time is a cancer. It steals blood meant for the heart. Chokes the life inside us. Victoria, you have this distressed look in your eyes. But I don't understand why. This is just how things go. We're all compelled to talk and untalk, draw and erase. Hurt and heal. Because inside a human being is where God learns, as Rilke wrote. It's been two years since Andre passed away. Good god. When you lose a symbol like that, you lose everything: your gravity, your sense of center. So we gather in the house he used to occupy, even though, inside, we only get further and further from everything that he meant to us—

CHLOE

I think some of us are getting closer and closer.

LEO

Hey man, why don't you go out the porch with me for a second—

CHARLIE

Leo, I know you look up to me, but you shouldn't: I'd betray you the first chance I got, just like I've betrayed everyone else, in one way or another.

LEO

I don't believe you.

ARTHUR

Oh fuck Leo: you're in love with him—

CHARLIE
There is nothing more seductive—and dangerous—than someone who's lost their hope.

LEO
Somewhere along the line I developed the habit of never saying what I mean, never standing up for myself. And the consequence is that I feel completely defined by what other people say about me.

CHARLIE
And what do people say?

LEO
Almost nothing.

CHLOE
Oh Leo...

LEO
I feel like, as the youngest, most unformed person in the room, I have to sacrifice my sense of identity to preserve everyone else's—

ARTHUR
Honey, you're just scared of who you are.

LEO
Everything you say is an attempt to humiliate me Arthur.

ARTHUR
No, I'm telling you the truth, so that you can grasp it for yourself—

LEO
Humiliation is how you were taught to be queer and so you assume it's gotta be that way for me too—

ARTHUR
Ok, that hurt for real.

    Enter Alana.

ALANA
Morning.

CHARLIE
Ok, I'm ready to go upstairs and talk—

Alana sits down and pours herself a cup of coffee, takes out her phone and begins to scroll.

VICTORIA
Go to hell.

ALANA
Does anyone else want coffee? I don't want to drink it all.

LEO
It's all yours.

ALANA
(looking at her phone)

Oh no—

CHLOE
What?

ALANA
Has anyone checked Facebook this morning?

CHLOE
No...what happened?

ALANA
Sophia died last night, in a car accident. People are posting about it on her wall.

   Silence.

VICTORIA
I told her that she wasn't welcome here, after Andre died.

CHARLIE
What?

CHLOE
This isn't your house—

VICTORIA
I'm sorry.

ARTHUR
Who's Sophia? Is she important or something?

VICTORIA

I'm sorry.

CHARLIE

At the end of the day, one person died, just like a six or seven billion more will before too long.

VICTORIA

I felt a kick...

LEO

I wish Uncle Andre were here.

CHLOE

I don't. Not for this.

ALANA

It was near midnight. We had a bonfire going; we'd had a few beers. I wasn't thinking. Neither was Catherine. I should have told her not to go swimming. I heard a feint shout: the sound of someone disappearing forever. Her body was found the next morning.

FRED

I don't know if I'm happy to be alive, but I'm grateful for it.

Gradual black out. Clear light.

Andre stands in front of his painting, admiring it.

Sophia reads on the sofa.

ANDRE

Most people think of life as an aesthetic problem and of death as a religious problem, but for me, it's always been the other way around.

"What would life be if we had no courage to attempt anything?" Van Gogh wrote in a letter to his brother Theo. It's a good question. What would life be? The same as it already is...insofar as none of us have the courage to live like Van Gogh did. Van Gogh, who hauled his imagination into the potato fields, or laid it at the feet of the swaying cypress trees and cried for joy.

"I feel that there is nothing more truly artistic than to love people," Van Gogh wrote, which is the truest thing an artist has ever said about their craft. Or about anything; life and death.

Andre goes and puts on the record of Mozart's Clarinet Concerto, the adagio.

Because it's true that no amount of suffering will buy our faults back. Consequences rain down on us and everyone we loved and love, unremittingly.

The future is there, ahead, flowing towards us; like a river running in reverse. What are we afraid of? That what's inevitable will eventually arrive?

We have to receive the mercy and sorrow of being a human being into the heart. We have a responsibility not to cower and to let ourselves be rained upon. To stand in the storm like Lear and cry for the kingdom that has been lost.

It's a perfect morning. A passionate morning. There is a flock of wild birds in the sky, almost invisible at the horizon. I do not have to go to the window to know that they're there.

Because I never thought I would be this happy; restored to the ardor in me—my nature, my light. Because I never thought I would be this happy: buried in the ground of memory…whose memory I cannot say—

And the dead, who fill the earth—they do not ask for much; only that we acknowledge them, for their dreams are our waking lives.

Because the mind is like a water-wheel, passing in a glimmering arc through river and air.

I think the painting is finished now.

And oh, my Soul, I think you are ready. I think it's time to begin.

I have had my vision.

FIN